# Megamouth!

# Megamouth!

James Stazzer

Illustrated by Mei Lim

**ELEMENT**
CHILDREN'S BOOKS

SHAFTESBURY, DORSET · BOSTON, MASSACHUSETTS · MELBOURNE, VICTORIA

To Beetle

© Element Children's Books 1999
Text © James Stazzer 1999
Illustrations © Mei Lim 1999

First published in Great Britain in 1999 by
Element Children's Books
Shaftesbury, Dorset SP7 8BP

Published in the USA in 1999 by
Element Books, Inc.
160 North Washington Street,
Boston MA 02114

Published in Australia in 1999 by
Element Books and distributed by
Penguin Australia Limited,
487 Maroondah Highway, Ringwood,
Victoria 3134

James Stazzer has asserted his rights under the Copyright, Designs and Patents Act, 1998, to be identified as the author of this work.

All rights reserved.
No part of this publication may be reproduced or transmitted or utilized in any form or by any means, electronic, mechanical, photocopying or otherwise, without the prior permission of the Publisher.

Cover design by The Design Group, Honiton.
Typeset by Dorchester Typesetting Group Ltd.
Printed and bound in Great Britain by Creative Print and Design.

British Library Cataloguing in Publication data available.
Library of Congress Cataloging in Publication data available.

ISBN 1 902618 36 X

# CONTENTS

**What's out there?**   7

**Roaming the Earth**   15

**Monsters of the deep**   33

**Dinosaurs –**
   **still with us after all these years?**   55

**Keep watching the skies**   83

**Hoaxes and Hollywood**   95

**Predictions and resurrections**   109

**Acknowledgements and further reading**   123

# CHAPTER 1

# what's *out there?*

MEGAMOUTH!

# undiscovered

**Surprising** as it may seem in a time of satellites, mobile phones and mass communication there are still many parts of the planet that human beings don't know that much about. 13,000 feet down in the depths of the mid-Atlantic, 5 days walk into the Likouala swamps of the Congo, deep in the gloom of the Vietnamese rainforest we still don't really know exactly what's out there.

When you look at the animal and plant kingdoms neatly labelled and set out in textbooks, it's easy to think that we know all there is to know about the other life forms that share the planet with us. Not so!

Only 150 years ago many of the animals that are the regular stars of today's wildlife programs were unknown to Western science. The people who lived in the same part of the world as these animals didn't always know much about them, either. Perhaps they had heard that some big creature with fangs was killing the goats in the next village, or that grandma too once saw a monkey with that funny striped tail. Of course, sometimes they knew these "undiscovered" animals well and had names for them. But scientists had not had the chance to see, and study, the animals for themselves.

The truth is that we don't even know approximately how many species there are on the planet. Because of the rapid destruction of the natural environment in species-rich areas like rainforests, several species become extinct every single day, many of them ones that have never been spotted or cataloged.

And yet the estimate of the

total number of species on Earth has gone up enormously in recent decades. Scientists now believe that there are maybe **13 million species**. So far, we have discovered about 1.7 million of them.

Most of the remaining millions of species will never star in those wildlife programs, though. One beetle or sparrow looks much like another, unless you're an expert. And some undiscovered creatures are sure to be microscopically tiny, maybe parasites that live in a particular bird's stomach. But a few of them are going to be new to science and very different. These are the discoveries that zoologists and cryptozoologists dream of making.

## Cryptozoology

Cryptozoology is the search for "hidden" animals. You can search for hidden animals in three ways:

# 1

You can go to a
remote and
inaccessible area and
start turning over
stones. Perhaps you'll
get a new species
of lizard named
after you.

# 2

> You can sit in a laboratory and look at DNA[1] samples. Perhaps you'll find that what you thought was one species of lizard is really two that look very similar.

[1] DNA is the genetic material in a cell, which contains the body's instructions for making the proteins out of which the whole creature is built.

WHAT'S OUT THERE?

# 3

You can collect reports and sightings of strange animals, form a picture of what you think is out there, and go and look for it. Perhaps you'll find the Loch Ness monster.

Just because something sounds far-fetched, that doesn't mean it can't turn out to be true. Earlier experiences have taught zoologists to be wary of dismissing reports out of hand. Sixty years ago a creature that was thought to have died out with the dinosaurs turned out to be alive.

In addition to the new animals being discovered, there are still plenty of strange tales and rumored sightings of other bizarre creatures. Welcome to the world of cryptozoology! It's a melting pot of hard science and mythical stories, one part fact, one part fiction. Could there really still be dinosaurs alive on the Earth? Could there possibly be an eight-foot-tall (250 cm) humanlike ape in the forests of America's Northwest?

With many of the wilder mystery creatures, hard science says that there is no chance. And it has to be admitted that cryptozoology *has* attracted more than its fair share of adventurers and fraudsters.

Then again, think of the scientists who've found a place in the history books by coming back with proof of their amazing discoveries. Somewhere out there, under the ocean, deep in the forest, holed up in a cave, there are still plenty of new creatures waiting to be found.

# CHAPTER 2

# *roaming* the *Earth*

## Legendary beasts

### Here be dragons

For as long as humans have been here we've been deeply curious about what else might be sharing our space. What's over the hill, round that corner, making that scrapy rustling noise in the back of our cave? Filling in the gaps in our knowledge has been a "stop start" sort of a journey: big discoveries followed by plenty of wrong turnings.

In the Middle Ages, people didn't like leaving big white spaces on their maps and admitting that there were parts of the world that they knew absolutely nothing about. So they decorated the unknown areas with pictures of fantastical creatures, or they just wrote "Here be dragons."

Unfortunately there never were any dragons in the known parts of the world.

Not until 1912, that is. That's when European scientists first made their way to the tiny Indonesian island of Komodo. The giant lizards they found living there (and on neighboring islands) look just like dragons. They are monitor lizards, and share an ancestor with the dinosaurs.

Over their 30-year lifespan, Komodo dragons can grow to a length of more than 10 feet (3 meters). The heaviest one on record weighed in at 366 pounds (166 kg), but that must have been right after a big dinner – Komodos can eat 80 percent of their own body weight at a single meal.

Once the scientists caught up with Komodo dragons in the flesh they found that, in this case at any rate, the dragon stories were actually true. The real-life dragons were every bit as fearsome and potentially dangerous to unwary humans as the rumors had suggested.

## Unicorns

Around 400 BC the Greek historian Ctesias wrote about the Indian wild ass. He described it as being about the size of a horse with a pale body and a horn 20 inches (50 cm) long set on its

forehead.
He added that
it was very fleet of
foot and hard to capture. Ever since then people have been building on that description to create the huge body of legend, myth and magic that whirls around that fabled creature – the *unicorn*. Down through history the unicorn was invested with extraordinary powers. Cups supposedly made from unicorn horn, but really fashioned out of rhinoceros horn or narwhal tusk, were treasured by kings and emperors in the Middle Ages as a protection against poison. Across the medieval world from Britain to China the unicorn appeared in manuscripts, tapestries and paintings.

Going back to that description from 400 BC though, many people think that what Ctesias was describing was probably an Indian rhinoceros. If that's right it's a wonderful example of just how much can be created from one animal sighting. The original rhinoceros was alive, and in the telling and the retelling the unicorn came alive too. Science can prove that no such thing as the unicorn existed but in people's minds and beliefs it was real and, to them, that was what mattered.

## Lost worlds

### Angel Falls

The more scientists discovered about the worlds of plants and animals the more people realized that "nature" was even weirder and more wonderful than they had thought.

Charles Darwin's theories of natural selection and evolution had burst like a bombshell in the nineteenth century and made natural history a hot subject. Novelists soon picked up on the possibilities, with fantastic tales of totally undiscovered places where evolution might have taken another course. When the author who created Sherlock Holmes, Arthur Conan Doyle, set out to write a new adventure story, he called it *The Lost World*.

It is the story of a scientific expedition to a remote South American plateau. What they find there is a world frozen in time since the age of the dinosaurs. The story was inspired by the Gran Sabana region in southeastern Venezuela. When Conan Doyle's book was published in 1912, this was still a blank spot on the map, and even today many parts of it have barely been explored.

Everything about this world is extreme. Plateaus rise thousands of feet straight up from the forest floor. The rock islands that poke up above the clouds are vast blocks of sandstone that were here when South America and Africa were still joined together as one huge southern continent. The sheer rock faces and the enormous height of some of these plateaus kept whatever animals might be on top in and outsiders firmly out.

It was only in the 1930s that people began to get a look into this lost – or, rather, undiscovered – world. In 1937 Jimmy Angel, an American pilot, crash-landed his plane on top of the plateau called Auyan Tepui and helped to put the world's highest waterfall on the map. Seen from the top, Angel Falls plunges 3,260 feet (978 meters) down to the forest below.

Since the first adventurers, scientists have been able to follow and begin the job of cataloging what is here. They haven't found any dinosaurs but there may still be many surprising animals to discover, hidden in the nooks and crannies.

## New Guinea – an island full of surprises

Tim Flannery, a research scientist at the Australian Museum in Sydney, has been exploring the world's second largest island since 1981. In its own way it's just as inaccessible as Venezuela's Lost Worlds – rugged mountain peaks splay out from a summit of 16,500 feet (5,000 meters) over more than 300,000 square miles (777,000 square kilometers) of dense rainforest and some of the wettest swamps in the world. Getting around in the interior is a complete nightmare which means for a zoologist this can be one of the most rewarding places on earth.

In 1981 there were some 200 species of mammal "on the books" for New Guinea. Eighteen years later, by crawling all over the island, Tim Flannery has added a further *twenty* species of mammal new to science. In the highlands he came across a new species of three-foot-long rat and, in 1994, the bizarre black and white whistling tree kangaroo. Real creatures are often far stranger than the ones we imagine!

## War-torn Vietnam

Between 1965 and 1969, the United States Air Force dropped 4.5 million tons of explosives on the fields, forests, mountains, rivers, and some of the towns of Vietnam. Each 500-pound (227 kg) bomb could leave a crater 30 feet (9 meters) across and 15 feet (450 cm) deep. On so-called saturation-bombing missions, strips of forest 1.5 miles (2.4 km) wide were turned to mud and matchsticks.

On top of the bombs, the Air Force also sprayed poisonous chemicals on a forest area bigger than

## Science

### Vu Quang Nature Reserve, northwest Vietnam, May 1992

Scientists were carrying out the first preliminary survey to see what animals might live in the dense forest high up in the mountains 220 miles (350 km) from the capital Hanoi. Whilst talking to local people the team came across an unusual looking skull hanging in a village hut. The hunter said the original animal was a type of mountain goat but the skull had straight parallel horns more than a foot (30 cm) long and it didn't look like a goat's skull.

The locals called the animal *sao la* which is the indigenous name for a weaving spindle, a tool that the villagers use which looks like the animal's horns. Once they knew that the scientists were interested, hunters produced other *sao la* "trophies." When the scientists left the forest they had 20 skulls and three skins but they hadn't found any trace of a live *sao la*.

### News

New York State to try to clear the tree cover that the troops fighting for a united Vietnam could hide beneath.

So you wouldn't expect there to be a lot of wildlife left in Vietnam. Let alone animals new to science.

### Searching for the sao la

DNA tests on the skulls and skins confirmed that the *sao la* really was a completely new large mammal. There was huge excitement. The only problem was that very few people had ever seen a live one. Hunters working in the Vu Quang reserve heard of maybe one or two being caught in traps each year.

There were good reasons why the *sao la* had eluded zoologists for so long. The animal lives in extremely steep, rugged terrain covered with thick foliage. And to make it even harder, it's active mainly at night. Picture a zoologist climbing sheer, rain-drenched rock faces and picking a way silently through dense bushes – all in the pitch dark. Suddenly he bumps into something large, warm and furry. Is it a *sao la*? Whatever it is, the creature is not going to stick around until daylight, and if he shines a light on it, it'll run off without posing for a photo.

The best chance of getting a live specimen would be in the winter months. That's when water in the highlands becomes scarce and the *sao la* come down to the lowlands.

## The giant muntjac

When the zoologists returned to the vast reserve to begin looking for the *sao la*, they had a by now familiar experience. While talking to hunters about possible sightings of *sao la*, they happened to notice more unusual-looking skulls decorating the walls of village huts.

They had stumbled across evidence of a second large and previously unknown mammal.

This time they were looking at the skull of an outsize muntjac, a type of deer. At this time, the largest muntjac in the world was thought to be the Indian variety, which stands about 2 feet (60 cm) tall at the shoulder. From the size of the skull, the Vu Quang muntjac had to be almost twice the size – a giant new species.

Now the scientists had not one but two shy and elusive creatures to track down. Eventually, in March 1994, a zoologist's efforts were rewarded. She had spent weeks combing the reserve, and now she was walking back to her camp in driving rain. Something made her look up, and there, ahead of her on the track, stood the beautiful silhouette of the Vu Quang muntjac.

The original cause of all the excitement, the *sao la*, managed to keep out of the scientists' clutches a little longer, until June of the same year.

Then a four-month-old female calf was trapped by a local hunter and taken into captivity. This animal became final proof that the *sao la*, also known as the Vu Quang ox, really does exist.

### And that's not all

Vietnam has also sprung other zoological surprises in the 1990s. In addition to the *sao la* and the giant muntjac, scientists have found:

▼ The smallest muntjac in the world, the Truong Son muntjac. It is known locally as *sam soi cacoong* – "the deer that lives in the deep, thick forest."

▼ A male and female pair of Edwards pheasants, thought to have been extinct since 1928.

▼ Three species of river carp and a loach that are all new to science.

## Ituri forests, Congo

The tropical forests along the banks of the Ituri River, right up in the northeastern corner of Congo, are remote and hard to reach. They lie 1,000 miles (1,600 km) inland, right in the heart of the African continent. To the east they are protected by a chain of peaks known in ancient times as the Mountains of the Moon. Few outsiders venture into these forests.

In the 1880s Henry Stanley, the explorer and journalist who found Dr. Livingstone, passed through here on his travels. He heard tales of a strange creature from some of the local people who were Pygmies and occasionally caught it in pit traps. It was big, over 5 feet (150 cm) tall and said to combine features of zebra and giraffe with a hint of antelope and mule thrown in. The Pygmies called it *okapi*.

Stanley mentioned the rumors about it in his 1890 book *In Darkest Africa.* It was enough to make zoologists and explorers in America and Europe realize that if the stories turned out to be true, the animal in the Ituri forests would be the most sensational discovery of a land animal for generations.

## *So near but yet so far*

Years later, another Westerner made it to the Ituri forests. He was an Englishman called Sir Harry Johnston. In 1899 he traveled with the Pygmies and spent months under the forest canopy hoping to see a real live okapi.

Finally the Pygmies showed Sir Harry fresh tracks which they said were unmistakably made by an okapi. Unfortunately the Englishman didn't take the local people's advice. Sir Harry was convinced that the okapi was going to turn out to be a member of the horse family and since these tracks looked more like those of a large antelope he turned away to look elsewhere. And that's why he never found an okapi.

Instead of leaving the forest with a live okapi, Sir Harry had to content himself with two bits of striped okapi skin. The skins were unique so at least they proved that the okapi existed but, as he was to realize later on, he had been within a few hundred yards of seeing a whole live animal.

***Meet the okapi***

Another ten years passed before a trained scientist could tell the world what the Pygmies of Ituri had known for centuries. An expedition from the New York Zoological Society reached the Ituri River in 1909. Eventually they caught two whole okapis.

Once they got a good look at one, what they saw

turned out to be even stranger than they had imagined. The central part of the body was covered with a velvety coat in a purply brown color. The rump and legs were covered in dazzling zebra stripes. A pale head rose from a longish neck. The animal had long ears like those of an ass and a blue-black tongue, about a foot (30 cm) long, which it could use to clean its eyes.

The okapi exceeded everyone's expectations. This was really something else, an animal different to anything people had seen before.

Once they had examined one, the scientists realized that the okapi was in fact a type of short-necked giraffe. Back when the planet was millions of years younger, there had been not one but several different types of giraffe, some of them specialized and adapted to live in the forest. Now, at last, the secret of the Ituri forests was revealed: a giraffe that everyone thought only existed as a fossil was alive and well, hidden in deepest Africa.

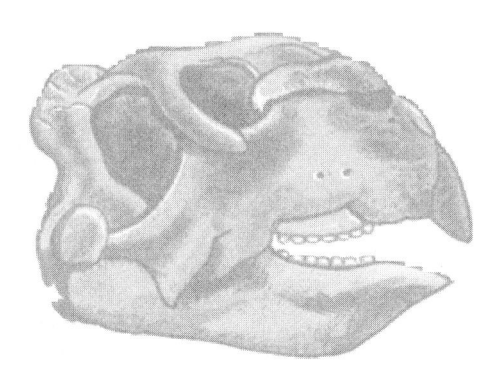

# CHAPTER 3

# *monsters* of the *deep*

**People** have always loved to scare and impress one another with tales of huge or weird animals. Our remote ancestors probably told such stories round their campfires on the savanna.

But were the earliest stories of fabulous beasts just stories, or could they have been descriptions of creatures that did once exist?

### Biblical beasts

The Old Testament has plenty of monster tales, and among them are some that many people feel could, allowing for a bit of exaggeration, be descriptions of real animals. Take the behemoth. It appears in the Book of Job (40:15-24) and the specification says its "bones are tubes of bronze ... [its] limbs like bars of iron."

If you read the description, it's a powerful grass-eater that lives in the marshes. It could be anything from a large ox to an elephant, or some quite different animal that is no longer with us.

Far scarier, though, is the leviathan. God describes this creature to Job with real relish (Job 41). The leviathan is a sea monster who "maketh the deep to boil like a pot." "His teeth are terrible round about," and "a flame goeth out of his mouth." What's worse, according to Psalms (74:14), it has more than one head.

According to Jewish legends, the behemoth will one day do battle with the leviathan. Our money's on the latter.

## The Kraken

### A monster with horns?

Shift forward a bit in time and the reports of mysterious creatures don't dry up. In a book published in Rome in the 1550s there are descriptions of unknown sea creatures just as vivid as anything the best horror writers could come up with today:

> *Their forms are horrible, their heads square, all set with prickles and they have sharp and long horns round about, like a tree rooted up by the roots: they are ten or twelve cubits long [15–18 feet/4.5–5.4 meters] very black and with huge eyes ... the apple of the eye is of one cubit [1.5 feet/45 cm] and is red and fiery-colored which in the dark night appears to fisher-men afar off under waters as a burning fire ...*

Pretty scary and even more frightening if you consider that the writer might be describing something that 16th Century fishermen really came across. Sightings of strange beasts in general and sea monsters in particular didn't go away, in fact they continued to become more common. 200 years later strange sea creatures were still with us and, in Norway at least, they had a name – the *Kraken*.

## 1752 Bergen, Norway – local bishop talks to sea monster eye witness

Erik Ludvigsen Pontoppidan, Bishop of Bergen, published his survey *The Natural History of Norway* and included in it detailed descriptions of the Kraken:

---

*Our fishermen unanimously affirm ... that when they row out several miles to sea, particularly in the hot summer days and expect to find 80 or 100 fathoms of water [480-600 feet/150-180 meters] it often happens that they do not find above 20 or 30 [120-180 feet/35-55 meters] or sometimes less. At these places they generally find the greatest plenty of fish ... by this they judge that the Kraken is at the bottom ... there are sometimes twenty boats or more got together ... [When] they find that the Kraken is raising himself near the surface ... they immediately leave off fishing, take their oars, and get away as fast as they can ... in a few minutes after they see this enormous monster come up to the surface of the water ... several bright points or horns appear which grow thicker and thicker the higher they rise above the surface and sometimes they stand up as high and large as the masts of middle-sized vessels.*

Curiouser and curiouser. As travel got easier, and communications improved, stories of encounters with strange creatures continued to increase. Either this meant that there were more sightings of unknown creatures or it meant that people's imaginations were generally running riot. Take the strange case of the U Boat and the sea monster:

After the First World War was over, a German newspaper, *Deutsche Allgemeine Zeitung,* carried the following report from George von Forstner, Commander of German submarine U 28:

---

*On 30 July 1915 our U 28 torpedoed the British steamer Iberian carrying a rich cargo in the North Atlantic. The steamer, which was about 600 feet long sank quickly ... When the steamer had been gone for about 25 seconds there was a violent explosion. A little later pieces of wreckage and among them a gigantic sea animal, writhing and struggling wildly, were shot out of the water to a height of 60 to 100 feet [18–30 meters].*

*At that moment I had with me in the conning tower my officers of the watch, the chief engineer, the navigator and the helmsman. Simultaneously we all drew one another's attention to this wonder of the seas ... We did not have time to take a photograph, for the animal sank out of sight after 10 or 15 seconds ... It was about 60 feet [18 meters] long, was like a crocodile in shape and had four limbs with powerful webbed feet and a long tail tapering to a point.*

---

What did the men of U 28 really see? Depending on your viewpoint, there are three main possibilities:

**1** They could have made the whole thing up.

**2** There could be some rational explanation for what they saw (maybe the *Iberia* was carrying a gigantic model crocodile?).

**3** The sea creature that they claim to have seen really existed.

Without a good photograph or, better still, a piece of the creature in question, many of these extraordinary accounts are dead ends for the would-be investigator. Asking more and more questions after the event is not necessarily going to settle it either way. With many of the stories it comes down to whether you personally find them persuasive.

Sometimes, though, as science progresses, we do get conclusive answers to some of the questions raised by these animal mysteries.

In the case of the Kraken, the truth was as startling as the original stories.

## Green eyes and tentacles

For another 120 years after the Norwegian stories of the Kraken, reports of **monstrous tentacled creatures** continued to surface. There were stories of ships being attacked and even sunk. When small sailing ships were lost unexpectedly, people blamed the Kraken.

There were eyewitness accounts of terrible battles at sea, a clash of the giants, where a whale and a kraken would fight, churning the ocean up until one or the other was defeated. The legend of the Kraken grew and grew – it was huge, it was vicious, it would attack ships unprovoked. In 1870 Jules Verne gave the Kraken a starring role in his bestselling adventure novel *20,000 Leagues Under the Sea*.

---

*I looked in my turn, and could not repress a gesture of disgust. Before my eyes was a horrible monster, worthy to figure in the legends of the marvellous. It was an immense cuttlefish, being eight yards [7 meters] long. It swam crossways in the direction of the*

*Nautilus with great speed, watching us with its enormous staring green eyes. Its eight arms, or rather feet, fixed to its head, that have given the name of cephalopod to these animals, were twice as long as its body and were twisted like the furies' hair. One could see the 250 air-holes on the inner side of the tentacles. The monster's mouth, a horned beak like a parrot's, opened and shut vertically. Its tongue, a horned substance, furnished with several rows of pointed teeth, came out quivering from this veritable pair of shears. What a freak of nature, a bird's beak on a mollusk!*

---

Only three years later, off the Newfoundland coast, two men and a twelve-year-old boy were out fishing from an open boat. Suddenly they were attacked by a gigantic tentacled creature. It wrapped its suckered arms around the fishing boat and only the quick actions of the boy saved them. He picked up an axe and hacked through the tentacles. The creature sank back below the waves and the fishers lived to tell the tale. But this time it wasn't just a tale they had to tell. In the boat with them was a segment of one of the huge tentacles.

It was 9 feet (270 cm) long. This was the first solid evidence that the Kraken might be real.

One month after this encounter, fishers on the same bit of coast did even better. They trawled up an entire dead specimen of a squidlike tentacled creature of giant proportions – 32 feet (970 cm) long – and more or less intact. This finally gave the zoologists their chance to examine one of these legendary animals in its entirety.

## The biggest yet?

One night during the Second World War a British trawler was anchored off the Maldive Islands in the Indian Ocean. One of the crew was up on deck alone, fishing. Looking over the side he saw something in the water:

---

*As I gazed fascinated, a circle of green light glowed in my area of illumination. This green unwinking orb I suddenly realized was an eye. The surface of the water undulated with some strange disturbance. Gradually I realized that I was gazing at almost point-blank range at a huge squid.*

---

According to the sailor, the squid stretched

the full length of the trawler, which was 175 feet (53 meters) long.

## The Giant Squid and the Kraken ... one and the same?

Once scientists got the chance to examine giant squid carcasses they realized they were dealing with a creature that could grow to an enormous size. Just the body of a giant squid can be more than 20 feet (6 meters) long. A giant squid has been found that measured 60 feet (18 meters) from end to end, and the whole thing weighed more than one ton.

At one end of the cigarlike body is an opening to the giant's mouth and a very sharp beak. Around the mouth are five pairs of arms. One pair are extra long and these are used to grab prey and bring it into the mouth. Scientists reckon that the squid uses its beak to tear up its prey into pieces. Then the bits are pushed down the throat by a long radula – a sort of tongue with teeth. Just past the mouth are the eyes – and what eyes! Each one can be 18 inches (45 cm) across which gives the giant squid the largest eyes in the animal kingdom. Taken all together the giant squid is a powerful and efficient predator capable of engulfing large prey in its tentacles and ripping it apart into bite size chunks. The more scientists found out the more accurate some of the old stories about the Kraken began to sound.

Giant squid do occasionally attack ships. In the 1930s a giant squid hurled itself at the hull of a Norwegian tanker, the *Brunswick*. The tanker proved to be too much of a mouthful and the squid was eventually killed by the ship's propellers.

Giant squid and whales *do* fight. A Russian whaling ship witnessed a mighty battle in 1965 between a 40-ton sperm whale and a giant squid.

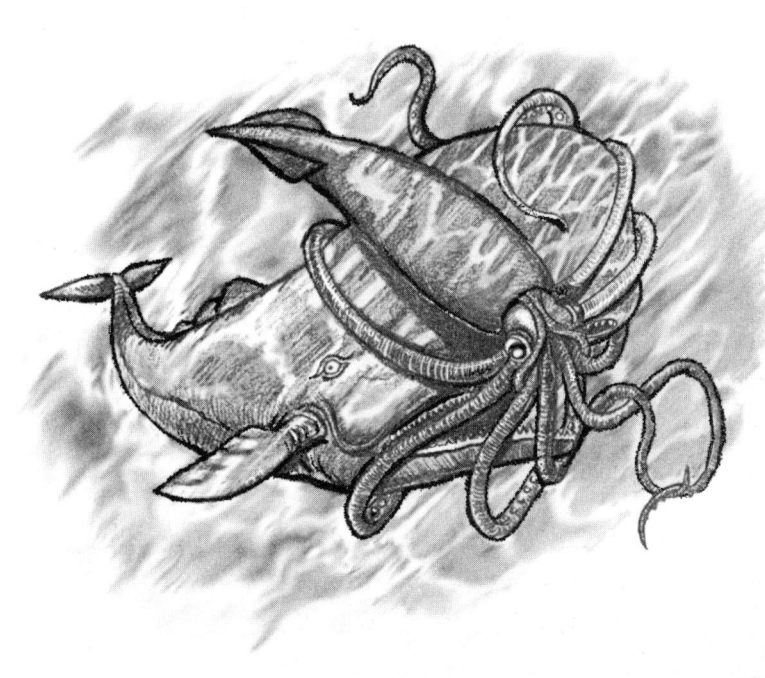

Both contestants died. The whale was recovered from the sea, strangled by the tentacles wrapped around its throat, and inside its stomach was found the severed head of the giant squid.

## Still a mystery

Although there are good reasons for thinking that many of the tales of the Kraken were probably based on encounters with giant squid, we still don't know much about these enormous and extraordinary hunters. They spend most of their lives hidden thousands of feet down in the deepest and darkest parts of the ocean. To date scientists have not been able to study them alive in their natural surroundings. Their knowledge is based on the few examples that have been caught at shallower depths or washed ashore.

Expeditions like the one in 1997 to Kaikoura, a deep undersea chasm off New Zealand's South Island, hoped to encounter real-life "Krakens" 6,000 feet (1.8 km) below the surface. That expedition drew a blank as far as these creatures went, but another search of Kaikoura canyon is planned during 1999. So we may soon know more about the giant squid – and who knows what else the researchers will find down there?

## Science

### Hawaii, November 15, 1976
### Megamouth comes up from the deep

A team of researchers from the Naval Ocean Systems Center were stationed 26 miles (42 km) offshore collecting data. In order to stop their research ship drifting too far they had two large parachutes which they used as sea anchors. While they were working the parachutes were lowered to a depth of 500 feet (150 meters) and when it was time to return to land they would be winched back on board.

Once they started winching, the team found that there was something large snagged in one of the parachutes. Although it was big and heavy, with the ship's equipment they were able to get it on board. After they had disentangled the parachute they found themselves face to face with an enormous shark quite unlike anything that any of them had ever seen.

The giant was 14.5 feet (440 cm) long and weighed over 1,600 pounds (725 kg). Some of its body looked like an ordinary shark but the head was radically different. It was huge and broad with an enormously wide mouth. The mouth had thick lips and hundreds and hundreds of tiny teeth.

When news of the discovery reached local journalists they rushed to see and photograph it and since so much of the new shark was mouth, someone coined the name for this new species – "Megamouth."

*News*

## Megamouth

Swimming in deep water, we may easily start worrying about what might be lurking underneath us, out of sight but perhaps not very far away. For scientists the ocean holds some of the last unexplored areas on our planet. Hidden below the waves there could be all sorts of living things – and we would never know until someone had a chance encounter ...

Since the discovery of the first one in 1976, only a few other megamouths have been found. But one that came to the surface off California in 1990 gave scientists the opportunity to find out how these sharks had avoided detection for so long.

The Californian shark was even bigger than Megamouth One – 16 feet (480 cm) long. It had got snared in a driftnet but was still alive. Scientists attached a radio transmitter to the shark and returned it to the sea. Then they sat back and tracked the signals.

The transmitter showed that during the hours of daylight megamouths stay deep, feeding on shrimps and plankton. The only time when these giant creatures leave the gloom of the ocean

## Science

### North Sulawesi, Indonesia, August 30, 1998
### Megamouth versus whale

A group of scientists studying whales in the seas off of Indonesia's thousands of islands came across an extraordinary event. Three sperm whales 33 feet (10 meters) long were mobbing an enormous shark. The whales swam off and the scientists were able to get close enough to see that the huge shark was a megamouth and only the 13th ever recorded. The shark appeared to be a bit dazed after the whales' attack and showed signs of bruising around its gills. After letting the scientists look for a while it rolled over and disappeared again back into the depths.

*News*

depths is after dusk. Then they will come up to feed nearer to the surface, but under cover of darkness, therefore the chances of anyone spotting one are very remote.

Even though we know they are out there, these sharks are so rare that in more than 20 years since they were first discovered very few people have been lucky enough to see one alive and in its natural surroundings. The Megamouth is still a mystery.

## Life in the planet's chemical cellar

Scientists know that the sea still hides many new and surprising creatures, but few discoveries have been as amazing as the clusters of new life forms discovered one and a half miles down where icy sea water and red hot lava meet.

Anything that lives down here has evolved to cope with total darkness, pressures of 2,900 pounds per square inch, and temperatures that can fluctuate from minus 1 to more than plus 80 degrees Celsius.

To us, coming from a surface world, where most life is based on energy from sunlight, the creatures of the *vent world* seem as alien as if they lived on another planet.

## Science

### November 1997, Atlantic Ocean, SW of Acapulco, Latitude Nine North

The American deep-sea submersible Alvin is stationed one and a half miles (2.5 km) below the surface. It's just above the ocean floor monitoring a vent site known as Nine North. This is the submarine that found the Titanic, 13,000 feet (4 km) down, so it's well equipped for the delicate work of collecting plant and animal samples from the edge of the vent where fresh superheated lava emerges to cool in the icy blackness.

### News

Scientists have known of the existence of vent worlds since 1977 when life was discovered on the sea floor 8,000 feet (2.5 km) below the Galápagos Islands. Since then the American deep-sea submersible *Alvin* has been making regular dives along the 46,000 miles (74,000 km) of the Mid-Ocean Ridge. This is where the tectonic plates that make up this portion of the Earth's surface separate. Along the rift, lava wells up and cools to form new material on the seafloor. Sea water seeps down through the new lava. As it gets nearer to the molten rock below the Earth's crust, it rapidly heats up and shoots back out through hydrothermal vents known as *smokers*.

## Chemical soup at the smoker

The water that comes back out of the vents can reach 350 degrees Celsius and carries with it a cocktail of acids, metals, and minerals collected beneath the Earth's crust. In the total absence of light, these chemicals are the energy source for dozens of unique life forms. Strange, powerful bacteria "crunch" hydrogen sulphide, iron, and manganese to make energy; larger creatures in turn harbor billions of bacteria and use their collective energy to grow. The chemicals are the fuel for a food chain that allows a bizarre collection of animals to call the smoker their home.

The most famous creatures of the vent world are the tube worms. They grow to a length of five feet (150 cm) and have vivid red flesh inside snow-white tubes. There are also white crabs, jellyfish, and giant clams 10 inches (25 cm) long, all of them quite different to their counterparts near the surface.

Life down there on the ocean floor is changeable and precarious. Vents can erupt, killing all the life around them. New vents suddenly open up. The smokers are sure to harbor many creatures yet to be discovered.

# CHAPTER 4

# *dinosaurs*
– still with us after all these *years?*

**Cryptozoologists** don't search only for new and previously unknown animals. Some of them are also obsessed by the possibility that creatures we know about, but believe to be long extinct, might in fact still survive, hidden in strange and secret corners of our planet.

With the help of reconstructions based on fossilized remains, we can picture what some of the beasts of the past looked like in all their glory. Unfortunately all the dinosaurs died out in the mass extinction at the end of the Cretaceous period 65 million years ago.

Or did they? What if one or two species survived?

What if somewhere in a murky swamp, on a rocky outcrop wreathed in mist, or lurking alongside the giant squid in a deep-sea trench, there were still a few surviving dinosaurs alive on the planet?

It couldn't happen, could it?

## Science

### South Africa, December 22, 1938

When Captain Goosens and the crew of the trawler Nerine pulled in their shark gill net, in it they found an extraordinary creature. It looked completely different to any other fish they had ever seen. It was 5 feet (150 cm) long, weighed about 130 pounds (60 kg) and was covered in fins and thick bony scales, and it had a huge mouth.

When they delivered it to experts from the local museum in East London they didn't realize that they were dropping a zoological bombshell on to the quayside. The giant creature was a coelacanth, a fish that had lived at the same time as the dinosaurs but which scientists were quite sure had been extinct for more than 80 million years.

*News*

Finding the coelacanth was a piece of luck. This particular fish was lost and far from home. It was later discovered that coelacanths normally live around the Comoros Islands, about 1,500 miles (2,400 km) from where the first one was found. And they tend to stay in caves and under overhangs at a depth of about 650 feet (200 meters), which is why they had escaped the notice of science for so long.

The discovery of the coelacanth rocked the world of zoology. It was considered impossible that such a fish could still be alive – but here it was. Fourteen years later another specimen was caught off the Comoros Islands. Since then, more have been found in that area and in Indonesia.

As it turned out, the Comoros fisherfolk had known about the coelacanth all along. They called it *kombessa* and used the fish's rough scales instead of sandpaper when mending their bicycle punctures.

The coelacanth is now officially endangered and may soon be extinct after all.

## If the coelacanth, what else?

The coelacanth proved that some of our strongest scientific convictions can still turn out to be plain wrong. It also showed what you may think is obvious: that local people who depend directly on the sea, the forest or the river for their livelihood often have far better knowledge of what creatures are living in their neighborhood than anyone else.

There are other, older examples of strange creatures from our past that still live on. Some 250 million years ago a whole mass of marine creatures with segmented bodies and jointed limbs disappeared off the face of the Earth. This was during the third great wave of mass extinctions. But one survived.

No one can be sure why, but the horseshoe crab, a strange armored beast with a smooth domed shield of a shell and a spiky tail, lives on. These crabs live deep down on the ocean floor, and the only reason we know they are there is that once a year for a few nights, when the moon is full and the tides are high, these prehistoric animals climb up onto a few particular beaches to breed.

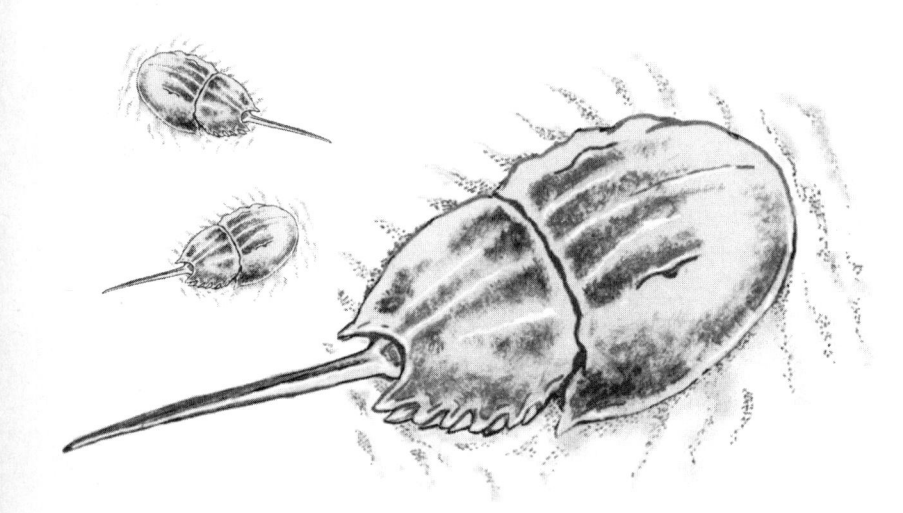

The continued existence of the horseshoe crab raises the hopes of cryptozoologists, some of whom really want to believe that there might be dinosaurs alive today, somewhere on the planet, waiting to be discovered ...

## Mokele mbembe – Africa's lost dinosaur?

### Likouala aux herbes, Congo, 1964

Nicolas Mondongo, a seventeen-year-old hunter, was standing on the banks of the Likouala aux Herbes River. About 40 feet (12 meters) from where he was standing, the waters of the river suddenly parted as a huge animal began to surface. Up came a very long, slender neck with a small reptilian head on it. Below this was a huge body on four stocky legs, ending in a long, tapering tail.

Nicolas was terrified but dared not move. For about three minutes the creature stayed on the surface. Then it slid back under the water and was gone.

Nicolas knew that the river where the creature had been standing was about 3 feet (100 cm) deep. Having seen nearly all of it out of the water from very close range, he could make a good estimate of its size. He thought the creature was about 60 feet (18 meters) in total length, of which about 6 feet (180 cm) was tail and another 6 feet was the neck and head.

Among his people, the Mbendjelle, who live in

the remote Likouala swamps in the Congo, the story of an elephant-sized creature with a long neck, a long tail and short legs has been passed on from one generation to another for a long time. They call it a *mokele mbembe*. Growing up in the village of Bandeko, Nicolas had heard the stories, but he had never seen one until that morning.

Nicolas' sighting was particularly vivid but it was not unique. His father had seen a similar creature, and around this part of Congo and up into Cameroon and the Central African Republic, there have been many accounts of meetings with large dinosaurlike creatures.

## Expeditions into the swamps

When Europeans first made the arduous journey to the remote Likouala swamps, local people were happy to tell them about the *mokele mbembe*. A German expedition to the area in 1914 documented many eyewitness accounts, but on their return to Europe the First World War had just started, and their report was ignored and eventually forgotten.

The Mbendjelle were sure that these animals were real. There were many accounts of their overturning boats and drowning people. In the time of their grandparents, a *mokele mbembe* was even reported to have been captured and killed by the men of one village. The villagers cooked it and ate it but, according to the Mbendjelle, everyone who ate the dinosaur meat died of poisoning.

In spite of the huge difficulties of getting around in the Likouala swamp, and the remoteness of the region, there have been several Western expeditions in search of the *mokele mbembe*. Zoologists, journalists, and writers have waded through the mud and been stung by the mosquitoes on the way to interview and re-interview the Mbendjelle, hoping to turn up more clues that might increase the chances of a sighting.

In the last twenty years zoologists have visited the exact places where *mokele mbembe* have been sighted; they've swum into riverbank caves and scanned lagoons using sonar equipment. They've examined and taken casts of three-toed footprints, analyzed giant droppings and lain in wait for day after day hoping to set eyes on a real Congo dinosaur or, better still, capture it on film. Occasionally one of the locals has reported a new sighting, but no one had managed to capture one of these incredible beasts on film until …

## Science

### A Japanese film crew fly over Lake Telle, September 1992

Director Mitsuharo Ondo and the crew of an expedition in search of mokele mbembe were flying over the swamps doing some reconnaissance prior to starting their search on the ground. The expedition's plane crossed over Lake Telle, an enormous body of water in the Likouala swamps. As they flew, they spotted something large moving along the surface about 100 yards from the shore. Out of the plane's window the cameraman recorded a few seconds of video film. This shows a long, dark, possibly dinosaurlike shape sticking up out of the water of the lake. Was this the first evidence on film of a living dinosaur?

The Japanese expedition eventually made it on foot to the shores of the lake but they found no trace above or below the surface of the creature they believed they had glimpsed from the air.

When the documentary of Mitsuharo Ondo's expedition was broadcast, Japanese viewers had to decide for themselves whether or not to believe that the few seconds of flickering images showed a real *mokele mbembe* captured on film. If you look at the footage it's hard to say. The picture is very grainy and the shape in the water is indistinct. There is nothing else in the shot to compare the would-be dinosaur with and, all things considered, the blurred shape could just as easily be a man bent over in a fishing boat as a wading dinosaur.

## So is there something hidden in the Likouala swamps or not?

The short answer is – we still don't know. The Japanese footage raised more questions than it answered.

There have certainly been many claimed sightings in the vast and sparsely populated Likouala region. If these creatures spend most of their time submerged, they could escape more definite detection quite easily.

As for the environment, this particular part of Africa has been relatively untouched by volcanic or climatic upheavals since the time of the dinosaurs.

On the other hand, 65 million years is a very long time for successive generations of a few very rare creatures to last. And in all this time no one has ever come up with a single piece of bone, claw, skin, or tooth that would give the zoologists something to work on.

Maybe there is a large, unknown creature in the Likouala swamps. Maybe the stories that the Mbendjelle tell are based on fact, and speak of a last survivor from the age of the dinosaurs. Or then again, maybe the *mokele mbembe* was always just a myth. Who knows?

## Nessie – the most famous dinosaur of them all

Stories of reptile survivors like the Congo dinosaur aren't that well known, but people have been talking about the possible existence of a Loch Ness monster for years. Even as far back as the

## DINOSAURS – STILL WITH US AFTER ALL THESE YEARS?

6th Century, when St Columba was meant to be converting Scotland to christianity, he is reputed to have met up with a monster in Scotland's giant loch. Now, 1,500 years later, whatever the scientists say, there are still plenty of Nessie enthusiasts. Some of them are convinced that dinosaurs – to be precise, plesiosaurs – are hiding in the loch.

## Science

### Loch Ness, NW Scotland, UK, July 22, 1933

George Spicer, a London tailor, and his wife were driving along the edge of Loch Ness when 50 yards ahead of them they both saw a creature resembling a dinosaur moving across the road. They stopped the car and stared. When it had gone out of sight towards the water's edge, they drove up to the spot. By the time they got there, though, there was no sign of the supposed monster. Interviewed on the radio, George Spicer described it as "horrible ... an abomination ... It had an undulating sort of neck quickly followed by a large ponderous body, 25 to 30 feet [7 to 9 meters] in length ... It crossed the road in a series of jerks ... I am certain that this creature was of the prehistoric species."

*News*

What Mr. and Mrs. Spicer saw was definitely real to them, but it was probably no more remarkable than other sightings reported over the years around the Loch. This time, though, thousands of people heard them being interviewed on the radio, and newspapers picked up the story and ran with it.

From here on, the Loch Ness legend began to get global attention. The "monster" soon became familiarly known as Nessie.

Soon afterwards, a rash of monster footprints appeared on the shore of the loch. On closer examination, though, it turned out that they had been made using a large ashtray.

## The Harley Street Surgeon and *that* photograph, April 19, 1934

Less than a year after the Spicers' sighting something else happened to make the Loch Ness monster front page news. Dr. Robert Wilson, a respected surgeon with a practice in London's Harley Street, produced a photograph taken at Loch Ness. He claimed to have seen a plesiosaur close up on the water. Plesiosaurs were marine reptiles from the time of the dinosaurs. They had long necks, short heads, and four large paddle-shaped feet. One of Dr. Wilson's photos showed the top of the creature's body above the water with a thick, long neck bent over at the top into a small head.

Ask anyone today to think of a mythical creature, a lost dinosaur, or any sort of animal-based legend and the image that will spring to mind will probably be this photograph. The image received enormous publicity and was reproduced in papers and magazines around the world. Whatever people might have seen or thought they had seen before, the idea was now firmly fixed in the public's mind: Nessie was a plesiosaur.

## So could there really be a giant relic from the time of the dinosaurs in the loch?

Loch Ness holds the largest volume of fresh water in the United Kingdom. It is about 23 miles (37 km) long and, at its deepest, it goes down about 790 feet (240 meters). It is connected to the sea at one end by the river Ness and at the other by sections of the Caledonian Canal and neighboring lochs.

The loch is an atmospheric place. If you look for long enough, you will see ripples on the surface of the water. Scientists will tell you they are seiches, which is the technical term for surface oscillations caused by differences in water temperature; these are found in most lakes, bays, and other partly enclosed bodies of water. But some people prefer to think that the ripples are caused by a giant flipper passing just below the surface.

Scientists argue that the Loch Ness monster couldn't possibly exist. These are some of the reasons:

- ▼ There isn't nearly enough fish in Loch Ness to keep a hungry Nessie going. The current estimate is that there are only about 20 tons of fish in the whole loch.
- ▼ Plesiosaurs breathed air with lungs, not with gills as fish do. If there were any in Loch Ness, they would need to come to the surface regularly to breathe. That would mean many more sightings.

▼ As recently as 10,000 years ago the Loch and the area around it were covered with ice. No long-lost reptile could have survived entombed in ice. So if there are mysterious creatures in the loch today, they must have swum in later from the sea. But that also means the species would have had to convert from being a salt water animal to living in fresh water. It would have been easier to swim back into the sea.

▼ And, of course, there is no scientifically proven evidence of plesiosaurs having survived anywhere else in the world. If Nessie's ancestors swam in from the sea, where are its relatives, the branch of the family that didn't emigrate to Scotland?

But no rational argument makes any impression on the true believers. If you're a die-hard Nessophile, probably the only thing that would shake you is if they drained the loch and there was still no sign of its most famous inhabitant.

## Still, there must be something in that loch?

A middle way between believing and disbelieving in a Loch Ness monster is a viewpoint that admits that people are seeing something out on the loch but puts less extreme creatures than a 50-foot extinct plesiosaur in the starring role.

Zoologists argue that there are actually quite a few candidates to choose from as Nessie substitutes. Since Loch Ness can be reached from the sea, quite large sea-going creatures do visit the loch from time to time. Seals have been seen occasionally and some people believe that a group of seals following one another near the surface could account for some sightings of huge multi-humped beasts rising up out of the mist.

Loch Ness has also had visits from a far stranger creature – one of the largest fish known to science, the Baltic sturgeon. These giants can reach 10 feet (3 meters) in length and weigh about 450 pounds (200 kg). They are bizarre, primitive-looking fish with a snout and large scales, and they have been known to migrate from the sea as far as 70 miles (more than 100 km) up British rivers to breed. Perhaps some of the Nessie sightings could have been a glimpse of this sort of "monster" instead.

## Looking for Nessie

For those who want to believe in Nessie's existence, encouraging evidence came from an Academy of Applied Science expedition in August 1972.

The team were exploring the dark depths of the loch, using echo-sounding equipment and underwater cameras. The echo readings showed shoals of fish swimming away from something large and solid that appeared to be following them. The equipment suggested that the solid thing was about 20–30 feet (6–9 meters) long.

When the underwater camera was recovered and the film developed, there were two images that caused huge excitement. Computer enhancement of the film seemed to show a diamond-shaped, pointed object about 4–6 feet (120–180 cm) long. Could this have been a shot of one of Nessie's hind flippers?

## A startling twist to the legend of the loch

The Loch Ness story can't seem to help being controversial. For those who always thought Nessie was just a myth the sensational death-bed revelation of a man called Christian Spurling was the final proof that they had been right all along. According to two researchers, David Martin and Alastair Boyd, the world famous photo of the Loch Ness Monster taken by the Harley Street Surgeon in 1934 was a fake.

The two men claimed that a model maker called Christian Spurling had confessed to them, just before his death in 1993 that the monster in the photo was actually a small model sea serpent mounted on top of a toy submarine. According to Spurling the whole thing was a hoax that got out of hand. The surgeon had gone along with it to make it more convincing and because he enjoyed a practical joke. Once the photo was published, the excitement and hysteria it caused made it too embarrassing for the men to reveal that it had been contrived to fool a gullible public.

Nessie fans dismissed the 1993 revelations as the misguided attempts of a dying man to discredit the most famous image of the monster. For them the photo is not a fake and the "revelation" cannot be proved.

In the end you just have to look at the evidence and make up your own mind. Wherever the truth lies, thousands of people still travel to Loch Ness every year to look for themselves.

## Where Nessie leads, other monsters follow

Nessie is definitely not alone. When it comes to deep-water mystery creatures it is only the most prominent among many:

## sweden

Lake Storsjön is the country's deepest lake. Since the 1600s people have claimed sightings here of a long-necked mystery beast.

## russia

Lake Brosno, 250 miles (400 km) northwest of Moscow, is allegedly home to Brosnie, a snake-necked creature spotted intermittently since 1854 and said to be up to 16 feet (5 meters) in length.

DINOSAURS – STILL WITH US AFTER ALL THESE YEARS?

# the united states

Lake Champlain lies between the Adirondacks in New York State and the Green Mountains in Vermont, and stretches up to the Canadian border. It is 109 miles (175 km) long and 11 miles (18 km) across at its widest point. Since the 1960s there have been many sightings of Champ – a brownish, long-necked creature about 30 feet (9 meters) long, usually with two or more humps.

# turkey

Lake Van in the east of the country, near the Armenian border, is said to be home to an aquatic monster with a long neck and horns. A video showing something that could be a humped monster was broadcast on Turkish TV in June 1997 – skeptics say it was just a tree or a strange-shaped rock.

# CHAPTER 5

# keep *watching* the *skies*

# monster birds

**For many** of us the idea that there might be large unknown creatures in the ocean depths or deep in some desolate swamp seems somehow more possible than the thought that there might be huge discoveries to be made in the skies above our heads.

In fact there are many reports of giant bird sightings, stories, and real-life accounts of children being carried away by monster birds of prey, and many cultures have myths of huge and dramatic birdlike creatures.

If extraordinary animals can evade detection below the water or deep in the forest, could huge birds do the same up in the sky?

## Could flying dinosaurs still be with us?

The dinosaurs' airborne equivalent were the pterosaurs. Most of the different species known from fossils were pretty dramatic-looking. Pteranodon, for instance, had a large crested head with a long, slender beak. Its wings were supported by a hugely extended fourth finger and the other fingers had developed into hooked claws. The wings were made of skin like a modern bat's. Because they

## Science

### San Antonio, Texas, February 1976.

Three schoolteachers driving along a little-used road near the Mexican border saw a huge shadow fall across the road in front of them. Looking up, they saw an enormous creature gliding just above them. Comparing it to the width of the road and their vehicle, they estimated it to have a wingspan of 15-20 feet (450-600 cm). The wings were gray and made from skin like a bat's.

The previous month a man living 150 miles (240 km) to the southeast, near Brownsville, Texas, heard a loud crash at night as something collided with his trailer home. He went outside and turned the lights on to see a terrifying apparition – a huge creature with red eyes, a long beak, and batlike wings, shrieking and backing away from the light.

had no feathers, they probably soared on air currents and glided rather than flew the way a bird flies. And they were big: a wingspan of 23 feet (7 meters) for an adult pteranodon was not unusual and one pterosaur skeleton, unearthed in Texas in 1971, measured 40 feet (12 meters) from wingtip to wingtip – about the size of a small plane.

We know from the fossils left behind that pterosaurs lived from around 130 million years ago to about 50 million years ago and then, like the dinosaurs, they disappeared – or did they?

Reported sightings of creatures like this, sounding a lot like pterosaurs, have continued to be reported in the United States. And not only in Texas – people claim to have seen them as far away as Pennsylvania in the Appalachian Mountains, 1,500 miles (2,400 km) to the north.

These pterosaurs were obviously quite real to the people who saw them; to everyone else they're a mystery. If only there was some hard evidence to look at ...

## The strange case of Arizona's big bird and the missing photo

In April 1890 a newspaper in Arizona, the gloriously named *Tombstone Epitaph*, carried a report of two ranchers who claimed to have encountered and shot a leathery-winged pteranodon-like creature up in the mountains outside Tombstone. According to the ranchers, the wingspan of the beast was a whopping 160 feet (nearly 50 meters). The newspaper report said that the men had cut off a wingtip as proof of their discovery. But nothing was done to follow up the claims or examine the supposed fragment.

The story of the 1890 sighting has become far more complicated over time and it has merged with the hunt for a remarkable photograph. In 1966, Ivan Sanderson, a famous cryptozoologist, had in his possession a photocopy of a photograph which reputedly showed an enormous bird nailed to a barn wall. In front of the bird were six men all wearing "cowboy" clothes. If the photo was genuine, could it be proof that some of these giant birds sightings were genuine? Ivan Sanderson is now long dead and cryptozoologists have spent years trying to track down the photocopy or even the original photograph. But so far no one has succeeded.

The last twist to the story came in 1970 when a very old man called Harry McClure, who claimed to have known the two ranchers back in the 1890s, gave his version of events. He said that the ranchers told him, at the time, that the creature had had a wingspan of 20–30 feet (6–9 meters) and that they had shot at it but they hadn't killed it. The creature had been left up in the mountains, perhaps wounded.

All of which leaves the rest of us somewhat confused. Did the 1890 "pteranadon" exist and was it killed? Could it possibly have been photographed? Each question leads to another question. Unfortunately, the trail of Arizona's big bird ran cold a long time ago; anyone old enough to remember who said what at the time of the first report would be about 115 years old today!

But possible pteranodons account for only some of the giants sighted in the skies of North America.

## The legend of the Thunderbird

The Thunderbird is a formidable creature that figures in many of the stories and images of Native North Americans. For generations of people, the Thunderbird was the physical representation of a powerful spirit that worked to ensure that rainclouds gathered and the grass grew. True to its name, thunder would be heard around the time that the giant bird was meant to appear.

Most images of the Thunderbird give it the appearance of a giant feathered bird of prey, similar to a massive eagle or vulture. Many people assumed that the Thunderbird was always just a legend but what if there *was* once a race of gigantic eagles? And what if some of their descendants were still alive ?

There are many legends and stories of children and even grown-ups being carried off by outsize birds of prey. One of the most famous features the Roc of the Arabian Nights, which flies off with Sinbad the sailor. But most Americans aren't prepared to believe in a modern day fairytale in real life. After all, birds don't really carry off children do they?

## *Science*

### Lawndale, Illinois, July 25, 1977

Ten-year-old Marlon Lowe was playing in the back yard with two friends when the three of them saw two enormous birds swooping down towards them. The birds seemed to be heading straight for them, so one of the boys dived into the swimming pool to escape.

One of the gigantic birds latched on to Marlon's vest with its talons and Marlon found himself being carried along about 2 feet (60 cm) off the ground. The bird carried him for about 30 feet (9 meters) and then dropped him.

Marlon's screams brought his mother and other adults running in time to see the boy being dropped back on the ground and the two birds flying off. They described the birds as being like giant vultures: they had black feathers, a white ruff around the neck, and wingspans of 8-10 feet (240-300 cm).

Was this a terrifying encounter with a modern-day Thunderbird or a fantastic story dreamed up by a few people? There was no physical evidence to go on; the alleged bird's talons had hooked on to the vest without scratching Marlon. Although other sightings of very large birds occurred elsewhere in the state, few people believed it could be true.

*News*

## Svanhild Hansen and the white-tailed sea eagle

Alongside all the unproven stories of kidnap by giant birds there is one account which has been thoroughly investigated and authenticated. In

1932, Svanhild Hansen, a four-year-old Norwegian girl was outside, playing near her parents' farm, when a large white-tailed sea eagle seized her in its claws. Carrying the girl, it flew off towards its nest some 800 feet (240 meters) up a mountain about a mile (1.6 km) from the farm.

Luckily for Svanhild, she was just too heavy for the eagle to carry her all the way to the nest. The bird dropped her onto a ledge 50 feet (15 meters) below the nest.

A group of villagers, following the direction of the eagle's flight, found her bruised and shaken, but still alive.

## Big birds, big mystery

For all the sightings and all the written accounts there is not much hard evidence to go on. There are undoubtedly some very big birds out there. An Andean condor has a wingspan of up to 10 and a half feet (320 cm).

Birds of prey do carry off large animals. A female harpy eagle in the Amazon was once spotted lifting a 13-pound (6 kg) sloth about 60 feet (18 meters) into the air. And, at least once, a very large bird has carried off a child who lived to tell the tale.

Whether this means that the Thunderbird might actually exist, or that the pterosaur encounters could have been with real creatures – still alive and living somewhere like the Mexican highlands – that's much harder to say.

# CHAPTER 6

# *hoaxes* and *hollywood*

**For as long** as there have been genuine searches for mystery beasts, surviving dinosaurs, and strange animals, there have also been individuals faking the evidence of a sensational discovery. Some do it for a practical joke, others hope to be taken seriously and get interviewed on TV.

## The Beast of Bodmin

Every year there are reports of alien big cats prowling around the British countryside. Probably the most famous is the mysterious Beast of Bodmin.

Many of the large cat encounters appear to have been with pumas or black leopards, but apart from inconclusive photos and videos – and a lot of dead sheep possibly killed by them – there is very little in the way of hard proof.

When a fourteen-year-old boy discovered a skull with large fangs in the river Fowey, on Bodmin Moor – home of the "Beast," – there was a great deal of interest in what the skull might reveal.

The skull was taken to the Natural History Museum

in London to be examined by experts and their findings were surprising. The skull belonged to a leopard. But it didn't follow that the leopard had therefore lived and died on Bodmin Moor. The skull also provided the experts with several clues to its origin, unintended by whoever put it in the river Fowey.

Inside the skull were tiny egg cases. Because of their shape and size, these could only have been laid by tropical cockroaches. The skull therefore must have come from a tropical country or have been stored in a place where tropical cockroaches could get at it.

The skull also had fine cut marks on it where a knife had been used to cut away skin and flesh from the bone. And the back of the skull had been cut away with something sharp.

Putting it all together the Natural History Museum were able to prove that *this* leopard definitely hadn't died of natural causes out on Bodmin Moor but the skull was probably put into the river as a hoax candidate for the title of "Beast of Bodmin."

## The father of all hoaxes: Piltdown Man

Anyone planning to fake an animal find could learn a thing or two from whoever was behind one of the nerviest frauds in the history of science.

In 1912 Charles Dawson created a sensation with his discovery of a skull in the Piltdown quarry in Sussex, southern England. The skull, with the jawbone found next to it, appeared to be exactly what scientists at the time most wanted to find — the missing link between apes and humans.

Most English scientists involved in the search for our earliest ancestors were enthusiastic about the find, but a lot of their American and French counterparts were skeptical. They were right to be suspicious.

The skull was in fact that of a modern human. It was only about 600 years old, and the jawbone was only 500 years old and came from an orangutan.

Someone had planted the two pieces next to each other in the quarry. They had also filed down some of the teeth to appear worn in such a way that the upper and lower jaw matched. The part of the jawbone that would have joined the skull had been carefully broken off, in order to hide the fact that the two parts could never have fitted together.

We still don't know whether it was Dawson or someone else who prepared the hoax, but they went to a lot of trouble to fool the scientific establishment. And it worked. Although Piltdown Man didn't fit in with other, genuine, discoveries, it wasn't until 1953 that the hoax was uncovered.

## The abominable snowman

Sir Edmund Hillary, the first person to climb Mount Everest, returned to the Himalayas in the 1960s. He spent considerable time looking for evidence of the yeti, the Tibetan word for the so-called "abominable snowman."

The peoples of the Himalayas have stories about a large shaggy humanlike creature sometimes seen in the mountains. They say it's a good 7 feet (2 meters) in height and covered in something like yak fur. Many locals and also some visiting climbers think they have seen its giant footprints in the snow.

In 1951 a photograph of one such footprint was published. That proved the yeti had to exist, then, didn't it?

In fact, you can make yeti footprints yourself, next time it snows. It works best on dark ground; try it on asphalt. Leave some ordinary footprints in a thin layer of snow early in the morning. Then go back after the sun has been shining on them for some hours. The snow will have melted around the edges of your footprint, making it look bigger.

Hillary made the same discovery. Following small animal tracks left in a shaded area by a fox or similar creature, he found that in full sun they melted and stretched to become huge, not to say abominable, "footprints" up to 20 inches (50 cm) long. What started out as fox tracks ended up as yeti footprints.

Sir Edmund's other finds turned out to be equally disappointing. A "yeti scalp" that he borrowed from a Tibetan monastery was carefully analyzed in the laboratory and found to have been made out of the moulded skin of a Himalayan serow – a goatlike animal. Yeti "fur" collected at the same time also proved to be a disappointment; it was fur but it came from the rare Tibetan blue bear. If the yeti was out there, these weren't the items to prove it.

## Bigfoot

If there was a prize for the mystery creature that the largest number of people wished existed, it would go to North America's Bigfoot, also known as Sasquatch. Most descriptions make Bigfoot an apelike creature 7–10 feet (2–3 meters) tall, weighing over 500 pounds (225 kg), roaming North American forests, especially in the Pacific Northwest.

In spite of the lack of scientific evidence to suggest that Bigfoot might exist in forests where logging continues to threaten the already known wildlife, every year hundreds of people set off to look for Bigfoot. So the number of claimed sightings continues to grow.

## A descendant of an extinct ape?

In 1935 a Dutch scientist called Ralph von Koenigswald visited a shop in Hong Kong that sold animal bones and skins. He bought a fossil tooth.

Much later he was stunned to discover that his purchase was a small piece of an extinct ape known as *Gigantopithecus blacki*. *Gigantopithecus* remains have since been found in China, dating back 400,000 years. Working from jawbones and teeth, scientists calculate that if *Gigantopithecus* were still alive today, it would be an ape standing about 10 feet (3 meters) tall and weighing over 1,000 pounds (450 kg).

*Gigantopithecus* is the fossil evidence claimed by many as the basis for sightings of apelike creatures right around the world. The yeti in Nepal, the Mapinguari of Brazil, the Yowie in Australia, and Bigfoot in North America could all, in theory, descend from this one giant ape.

Starting from Asia, *Gigantopithecus* could have migrated, possibly crossing into North America when the two continents were still connected by the Bering Land Bridge. From here, it's a small step down from Alaska to the forests of Canada and the United States.

The only problem is: *if* all that happened, there is still no conclusive proof to show that they really are still out there.

## The mystery creature that won't go away

Bigfoot has been a part of North American life for thousands of years. The Salish people of what is now British Columbia gave the creature the name Sasquatch, meaning "wild man of the woods." Native Americans living along the banks of the Columbia River in Oregon left behind carvings of man-beasts with an apelike face.

Fast forward to the 1840s. Pioneers and missionaries moving into the West thought they heard ape giants crashing about in the forest, often at night. Some even claimed to have glimpsed one. And it made a basis for good stories.

The name Bigfoot came later, in the 1950s, around the time the media got hold of the story. After that, of course, Bigfoot wouldn't go away. The old problem was still there, though: no real evidence. That was until ...

## Science

### Bluff Creek, Northern California, October 20, 1967

Roger Patterson and Bob Gimlin were searching on horseback for any sign of Bigfoot. Rounding a large obstacle in the dry riverbed, Patterson's horse suddenly reared up and the two men saw a large apelike figure striding across a sandbar about 90 feet (30 meters) away. Patterson had come prepared: in his saddlebag he had a 16-mm movie camera. Quickly he dug this out and ran after the creature, shooting off 900-odd frames of color film.

The film shows the creature moving away, walking upright, and at one point turning to look back at its pursuer.

At last: evidence on film to *prove* that what all those people had seen out there was no figment of their imagination but a real live ape.

On the face of it, film evidence should have reduced the mystery around Bigfoot – in fact it increased it. The film caused a huge amount of controversy. What it boiled down to was an argument about whether or not the figure in the film was a real ape, the missing Bigfoot, or a man dressed up in an ingenious ape costume.

For the last 30 years experts on ape skeletons and anatomy have argued over the film frame by frame. Some say the movements of the figure in the film are genuinely those of an ape, others insist that although it looks good, the whole ape outfit could have been put together professionally to look like the real thing from a distance.

## A contribution from Hollywood?

Not too far away from Bluff Creek and the mystery creature sighting are the studios and make-up specialists of America's movie capital – Hollywood. At *exactly* the time of the Patterson film, many of the top special-effects and make-up artists of the day were working on the series of sci-fi *Planet of the Apes* movies. These movies used state-of-the-art models and suits to create the most convincing moving apes. Many people in the movie business believe that the creature in Bluff Creek was really made in Hollywood – simply an actor in a brilliantly-designed ape suit.

Roger Patterson died in 1972. He had always insisted that he hadn't been involved in any hoax and was himself convinced that the "creature" was real.

Bob Gimlin, too, protested his innocence. In an interview in 1999 he was still insisting that their account of what they *saw* in 1967 was totally genuine, although he was prepared to accept that they could have been the innocent victims of a hoax.

And Bigfoot? For thousands of North Americans, whatever the experts say about the Patterson film or the lack of evidence, a real living Bigfoot is still out there for them, the elusive and charismatic "wild man of the woods."

# CHAPTER 7

# *predictions* and *resurrections*

**Instead** of climbing steep and slippery mountains, sweating in the rainforest, or freezing in the Himalayas looking for undiscovered creatures or possible survivors of animals that are thought to be extinct, some scientists choose to do their research in the comfort of the laboratory. But how far can lab-work go, and how successful could scientists be at bridging the gap between past and present? Could they, for example, provide the tools to re-create animals that disappeared long ago?

## Bringing dinosaurs back to life?

The idea behind the novel *Jurassic Park*, and the movie based on it, was that fossilized DNA could be isolated and used to produce live dinosaurs.

Think back to a fine day 66 million years or so ago. The scene is a steamy swamp with high ferns and buzzing mosquitoes. One brave and hungry mosquito bites a dinosaur and sucks up some of its blood. On a full stomach, the mosquito flies off and lands on a tree. The tree bark is sticky with oozing resin and the mosquito, with the dinosaur blood still undigested in its stomach, becomes trapped.

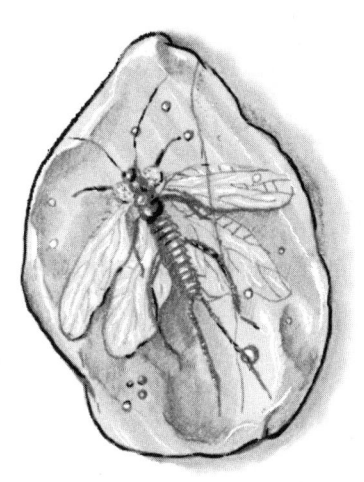

Let us not dwell on the lonesome death of the mosquito as it sinks into the resin.

Over the next many thousands of years, the resin becomes fossilized and turns into amber.

Zoom forward in time to the twentieth century. That piece of amber has found its way into a laboratory. Zoologists like to study insects trapped in amber. Some are much the same as today's insects, but others belong to more primitive species. Sometimes scientists can also identify the contents of the insects' stomachs, which tell them more about the world of the dinosaurs.

Our mosquito is carefully removed from the surrounding amber and the scientists extract fossilized dinosaur blood from its stomach. The dinosaur blood contains fragments of the dinosaur's genetic blueprint, the DNA. The fragmented DNA is then reworked into a complete copy of the dinosaur's DNA. And from it, hey presto, a live, full-size dinosaur is grown in the laboratory. Sounds pretty easy and it makes for a great story, but could it ever be done?

## Science catches up with Jurassic Park?

In the latter half of the 1990s, several separate groups of scientists working in America claimed success in extracting insect, plant, and bacterial DNA from amber up to 120 million years old.

Nobody can be quite sure what they are dealing with in this sort of research. To reduce risks, even the air in the laboratory may be filtered and all equipment sterilized to prevent the accidental release back into the world of some long-dormant plague.

In some of the American experiments, microbe-sized spores from a 25-million-year-old bee's stomach were transferred into a nutrient jelly. According to the scientists, within a few weeks they had prehistoric bacteria growing in a secure vault.

But could they have grown a prehistoric bee?

## The definitive answer – for now

Zoologists from the UK's Natural History Museum have been working since 1996 with ancient amber samples trying to extract DNA from creatures fossilized in the amber. Dr. Jeremy Austin is one of the zoologists from the museum's team. He has extracted DNA successfully from the remains of extinct lizards and tortoises. But these have not been anything like as old as dinosaurs.

According to Dr. Austin, the DNA recovered from 65 million years ago and even from much younger and better preserved material is degraded into very small pieces. To re-create a whole animal, you'd need long intact strings of DNA.

In his own words: "Cloning a complete organism from these small amounts of degraded DNA is impossible at present and I believe will always be impossible."

So there you have it! If we can't find a plesiosaur out in the wild, it's no good expecting the scientists to make one in the laboratory any time soon.

## A new life for the quagga

Even if dinosaurs can't be recreated, studying DNA has helped with a remarkable project: an attempt to *breed* an animal back into existence that became extinct 116 years ago.

When quaggas were alive they were a type of wild horse. In appearance their front half was striped like a zebra and the back half had few or no stripes, like a horse. Although they were once common in southern Africa, millions of quaggas were shot during the 1800s, until by the 1880s only a very few were left alive.

On August 12, 1883 the only quagga in the collection of Amsterdam Zoo died. No one realized it at the time, but that animal had in fact been the last quagga in existence. The whole species of quagga had slipped quietly into extinction.

## Unzipping its genes

Some eighty years later, Reinhold Rau, head taxidermist at the South African National Museum, was studying some quagga skins. He realized that one of them had not been properly preserved and that attached to the skin were some pieces of flesh.

A few years later, genetic techniques had developed sufficiently for scientists in California to extract fragments of quagga DNA from those pieces of flesh.

## The quagga's cousins

When the quagga DNA was compared to the DNA of certain types of plains zebras, the scientists found, to their surprise, that it matched. This meant that these zebras were the equivalent of cousins to the quagga. The zebras carried some of the quagga genes alongside their own.

If the right zebras could be selected and bred together, it was just possible that within a few generations the scientists would end up with a live, newborn quagga.

The quagga project has been running in South Africa since 1987. Although the animals being born now are only the grandchildren of the first zebras selected, already they are browner, have fewer stripes than normal zebras, and are beginning to look more like proper quaggas. In this case, at least, it seems there's a good chance of resurrecting a long-lost animal.

## Spotting new animals in the lab

In the search for new or "lost" animals, sometimes sitting and thinking can be just as useful as charging around the bush trying to catch yourself something. Some of the best discoveries by zoologists have been made back at base, in the museum or the laboratory once the dust has settled and the scientists have had time to start interpreting the evidence in front of them.

## The Bonobo chimpanzee comes out of the museum

One of the last large mammals discovered by science wasn't found in its natural surroundings by someone who had spent months trying to track it down; it was found by accident in the vaults of a museum in Belgium.

In 1929 in the Congo Museum at Tervuren, Belgium, a German anatomist named Ernst Schwarz was studying some chimpanzee skeletons and skins that were in the museum's collection. He was looking at a small skull which had been labelled "young chimpanzee" because of its size. The more he looked, the more he began to think that what he was holding wasn't the skull of an immature animal at all, but might in fact be the skull of an adult chimpanzee of a completely different species.

When he compared it with the remains of other chimpanzees in the museum, Ernst Schwarz realized that the shape of the skull and the appearance of the fur of this specimen were very different. He checked in the archive and found that the skull he had been looking at had been collected from the south of the huge Congo River, whereas all the other chimpanzees had come from the north.

The next expedition to the south of the Congo River had a good look at the chimpanzees there and, sure enough, there was reason to classify them as a separate species. Now known as the Bonobo (sometimes called the pygmy chimpanzee), it is a very different animal in its looks and behavior to the common species of chimpanzee. And since chimpanzees are our closest relatives, it is important to know as much about them as possible.

The Bonobos have a social structure where individuals have more equality than in other chimpanzee societies, and they are good at solving conflicts between members of the group.

Dr. Schwarz's initial detective work led to the Bonobo being classified and studied as a quite separate species, and the whole discovery was triggered by a chance encounter with a dead animal some 4,000 miles away from its natural home.

## The "I told you so" hawk moth

In 1862, Charles Darwin, the scientist who came up with the theory of evolution through natural selection, was studying orchids collected from the island of Madagascar. One of the species had a very deep, narrow flower. Having examined it, Darwin said that the flower could be fertilized only by a moth with an exceptionally long tongue. Since the flower existed, the moth must exist, even though no one had ever seen such a moth on Madagascar.

Darwin's prediction came good 41 years later. In 1903 the giant hawk moth, with a very long tongue, was found. It was given the Latin name *Xanthopan morgani praedicta* – the *praedicta* part referring to Darwin's foreknowledge of its existence.

## Still looking

The more we discover, the more we realize how much we don't know. Our understanding of what's out there and our knowledge of the rest of life on our planet, apart from ourselves, has developed in fits and starts. Most of the time we've been surprised by what's turned up; only on a few occasions have we been able to predict it.

Technology is helping. In the sea, zoologists have been using "critter cams" – cameras attached to living creatures like whales – as a new way of finding things in the most secret parts of the ocean, and learning more about what goes on there. In remote forests, pressure-sensitive mats and infrared beams trigger cameras that catch the images of animals passing by night. Ideally, new and exotic creatures will leave behind a snapshot of themselves.

There are plenty of animals left to find, judging by the rumors and sightings that are still coming in: giant cobras 65 feet (20 meters) long in the Amazon ... a new hairy ape in the forests of Indochina ... killer worms 2 feet (60 cm) long in the Gobi Desert ...

Many of these supposed creatures will be impossible, inconceivable, illogical, irrational, and generally completely out of the question, but the world is *exceedingly* big and *stranger things* have happened so ...

**you never know.**

**CHAPTER 8**

# *acknowledgements* and *further reading*

## Books

I have found the following books a source of inspiration, ideas and information. And they would be of interest to anyone wanting to read further.

---

Bille, Matthew A., *Rumours of Existence: Newly Discovered, Supposedly Extinct and Unconfirmed Inhabitants of the Animal Kingdom* (Blaine: Hancock House 1995)

---

Flannery, Tim F., *Throwim Way Leg: An Adventure* (Grove Atlantic 1999)

---

Hall, Mark A., *Thunderbirds! The Living Legend of Giant Birds* (Bloomington 1988)

## ACKNOWLEDGEMENTS AND FURTHER READING

Heuvelmans, Dr. Bernard, *In the Wake of Sea-Serpents* (London: Rupert Hart Davis 1968)

Heuvelmans, Dr. Bernard, *On the Track of Unknown Animals* (London: Kegan Paul International 1995)

Mackal, Roy, *A Living Dinosaur? In Search of Mokele Mbembe* (Leiden: E. J. Brill 1987)

Shuker, Dr. Karl, *In Search of Prehistoric Survivors: Do Giant 'Extinct' Creatures Still Exist?* (London: Blandford 1995)

Shuker, Dr. Karl, *The Lost Ark: New and Rediscovered Animals of the 20th Century* (London: HarperCollins 1993)

## Internet links

These are just a few of many sites that deal with cryptozoology and animal discoveries:

### Cryptozoological Realms

http://members.aol.com/mokele.crytozoological_realms/html_3.2/english/table-of-contents.html

### Natural History Museum, London

http://www.nhm.ac.uk/

## internet

### X Creatures – site of a BBC series on cryptozoology and mystery animals

http://www.bbc.co.uk/xcreatures/ark.shtml

### Kaikoura expedition and the search for the giant squid

http://www.nationalgeographic.com/features/97/kaikoura/index.html